W9-BWP-469

Community Workers

Keeping You Safe

A Book About Police Officers

Ann Owen
Illustrated by Eric Thomas

Thanks to our advisers for their expertise, research, knowledge, and advice:

Officer James Caauwe, Bloomington (Minnesota) Police Department

Susan Kesselring, M.A., Literacy Educator
Rosemount-Apple Valley-Eagan (Minnesota) School District

PICTURE WINDOW BOOKS
Minneapolis, Minnesota

Managing Editor: Bob Temple
Creative Director: Terri Foley
Editor: Peggy Henrikson
Editorial Adviser: Andrea Cascardi
Copy Editor: Laurie Kahn
Designer: John Moldstad
Page production: Picture Window Books
The illustrations in this book were prepared digitally.

Picture Window Books
151 Good Counsel Drive
P.O. Box 669
Mankato, MN 56002-0669
1-877-845-8392
www.picturewindowbooks.com

Copyright © 2004 by Picture Window Books
All rights reserved. No part of this book may be reproduced without written permission from the publisher.
The publisher takes no responsibility for the use of any of the materials or methods described in this book,
nor for the products thereof.

Printed in the United States of America.

All books published by Picture Window Books
are manufactured with paper containing at least
10 percent post-consumer waste.

Library of Congress Cataloging-in-Publication Data
Owen, Ann, 1953–
Keeping you safe : a book about police officers / written by Ann Owen ; illustrated by Eric Thomas.
p. cm. — (Community workers series)
Summary: Describes some of the things that police officers do to help keep people safe.
Includes bibliographical references and index.
ISBN 978-1-4048-0089-2 (hardcover)
ISBN 978-1-4048-0483-8 (paperback)
1. Police—Juvenile literature. [1. Police. 2. Occupations.]
I. Thomas, Eric, ill. II. Title. III. Community workers (Picture Window Books)
HV7922 .O9 2004
363.2'023—dc21

2003004165

Many people
in the community
have jobs helping others.

What do
police officers do?

A police officer teaches us when to call 9-1-1

and to be careful around strangers.

A police officer walks down the street

or drives a patrol car.

Some police officers ride horses.

Some police officers teach bicycle safety.

Police officers work with partners.

Some police officers have police dogs as partners.

A police officer helps you if you get lost.

Don't worry. We'll find your mom.

A police officer makes
sure everyone is okay

and takes notes about what happened.

Police officers look for clues.

Here are some fingerprints.

A police officer speeds to the scene

and catches people who break laws.

Police officers help keep us safe.

Did You Know?

- The first city in America to have a police force was Boston, Massachusetts. The force was started there almost 300 years ago.

- Boston, Massachusetts, and Chicago, Illinois, were the first cities in America where police officers wore uniforms.

- Lola Baldwin was the first female police officer. She joined the Portland, Oregon, police force almost 100 years ago.

- People disagree on the origin of the nickname "cop" for a police officer. Some think the name came from the fact that police badges used to be made of copper. Others say the name was created from the English term constable on patrol. A third opinion is that "cop" comes from a very old word that means to catch or capture.

- Police officers who work with police dogs are said to work "in K-9." This term comes from the word *canine,* which means having to do with dogs. *Canine* is pronounced like K-9.

A Police Officer's Equipment

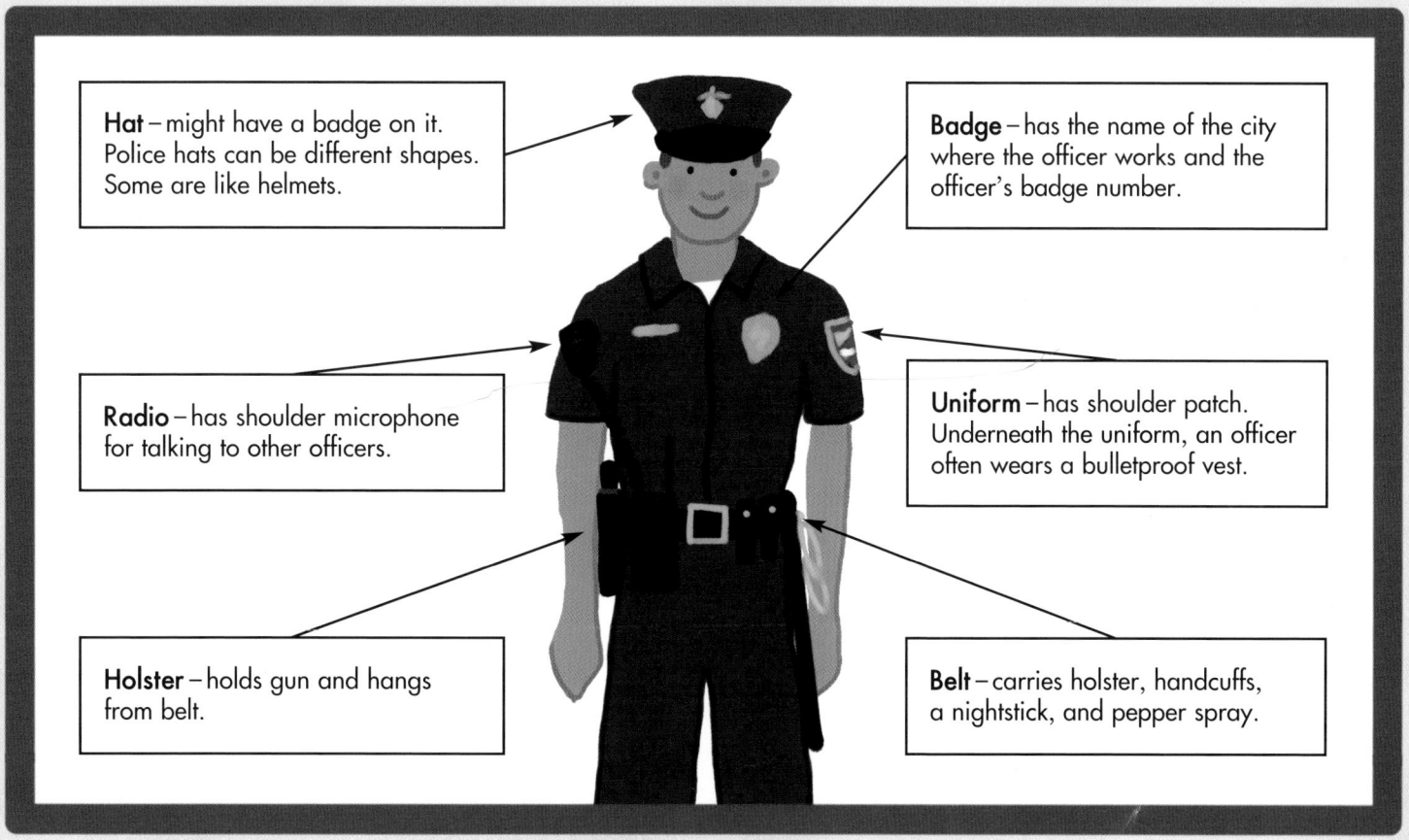

Words to Know

badge (BAJ) – a small sign with a picture, name, or other information on it that is pinned to a person's clothing. Police badges are metal and may be different shapes. A police badge often looks like a shield.

community (kuh-MYOO-nuh-tee) – a group of people who live in the same area

fingerprint (FING-gur-print) – a print made by the pattern of lines on the tip of a person's finger. By checking for fingerprints at the scene of a crime, police officers can sometimes find out who committed the crime.

law (LAW) – a rule made by a government

patrol car (puh-TROLL KAR) – the car a police officer uses at work

pepper spray (PEP-ur SPRAY) – a spray that makes people's eyes itch. Police officers use pepper spray to protect themselves.

police force (puh-LEESS FORSS) – the group of police officers in a town or city

safe (SAYF) – free from harm

To Learn More

More Books to Read

Flanagan, Alice K. *Police Officers*. Minneapolis: Compass Point Books, 2000.
Hayward, Linda. *A Day in the Life of a Police Officer*. New York: Dorling Kindersley Pub., 2001.
Liebman, Daniel. *I Want to Be a Police Officer*. Toronto: Firefly Books, 2000.
Ready, Dee. *Police Officers*. Mankato, Minn.: Bridgestone Books, 1997.
Schaefer, Lola M. *We Need Police Officers*. Mankato, Minn.: Pebble Books, 2000.

On the Web

FactHound offers a safe, fun way to find Web sites related to this book.
All of the sites on FactHound have been researched by our staff.

1. Visit *www.facthound.com*
2. Type in this special code: 1404800891.
3. Click on the FETCH IT button.

Your trusty FactHound will fetch the best sites for you!

Index

bicycles, 9
clues, 16–17
cops, 22
equipment, 23
horses, 8
K-9, 22
laws, 19
partners, 10–11
patrol car, 7
police dogs, 11, 22
uniforms, 22, 23